**Tuning In**

The Ambulance Service can be read from be[ginning]
may be more appropriate to read selected [sections]
notes take account of this.

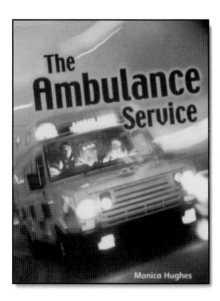

The front cover

Read the title.

What do you know about the ambulance service?

The back cover

Read the blurb. What is this book going to tell us?

Contents

Read the contents. Now read the index on page 16.

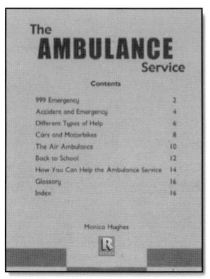

The
AMBULANCE
Service

Contents

Monica Hughes

Speaking and Listening

Using the information in the contents and index we can make a mind map (spidergram) for each section of the book.

Let's make a mind map (spidergram) of what you already know about each section.

Now let's choose one part of the mind map and we can use either the contents or the index to find more information.

READ

Read pages 2 and 3

Purpose: to find out if there is any more information to add to the mind map.

EXPLORE

Pause at page 3

Is there any information on this page that we have not put down in our mind map?

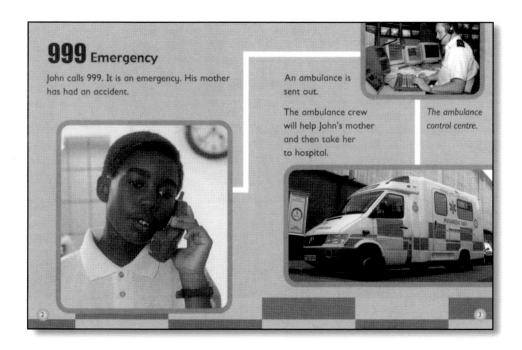

999 Emergency

John calls 999. It is an emergency. His mother has had an accident.

An ambulance is sent out.

The ambulance crew will help John's mother and then take her to hospital.

The ambulance control centre.

3

READ

Read pages 4 and 5

Purpose: to find out if there is any more information
to add to the mind map.

EXPLORE

Pause at page 5

Is there any information on this page that we have not
put down in our mind map?

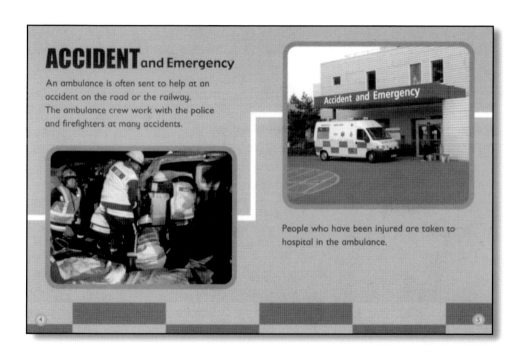

ACCIDENT and Emergency

An ambulance is often sent to help at an accident on the road or the railway. The ambulance crew work with the police and firefighters at many accidents.

People who have been injured are taken to hospital in the ambulance.

READ

Read pages 6 and 7

Purpose: to find out if there is any more information to add to the mind map.

EXPLORE

Pause at page 7

What information can we add to our mind map?

Where will you find the two words written in bold type? Look in the glossary on page 16 to check their meaning.

Speaking and Listening

Why would people need to go to day centres?

Different Types of **HELP**

The Ambulance Service does not only help in accidents and emergencies. Ambulances are used every day to take people to and from hospital appointments, to **clinics** and **day centres**.

A transport ambulance is like a minibus and can carry several people.

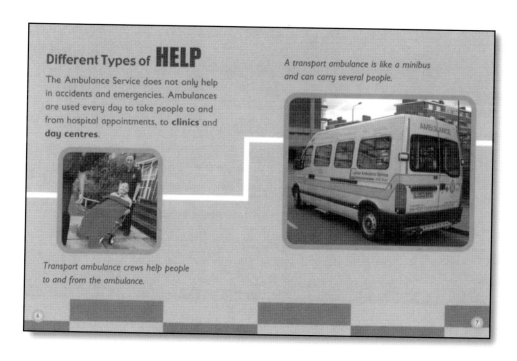

Transport ambulance crews help people to and from the ambulance.

6

READ

Read pages 8 and 9

Purpose: to find out if there is any more information to add to the mind map.

EXPLORE

Pause at page 9

Is there any information on this page that we have not put down in our mind map?

Speaking and Listening

Look at the heading.

How could you turn the heading into a question?

What would be the answer to the question?

Tricky word (page 8):
The word 'patient' may be beyond the children's word recognition skills. Tell this word to the children.

CARS and Motorbikes

The Ambulance Service sometimes sends cars or motorbikes to accidents and emergencies. A **paramedic** in a car can help a patient and also take them to hospital.

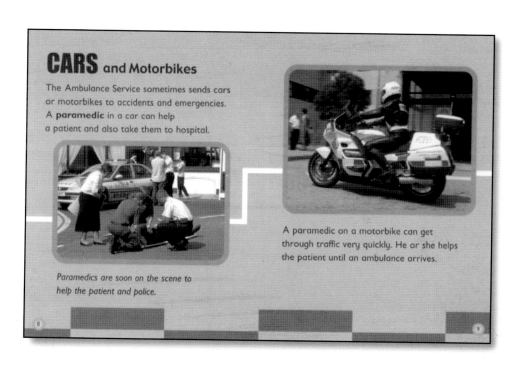

Paramedics are soon on the scene to help the patient and police.

A paramedic on a motorbike can get through traffic very quickly. He or she helps the patient until an ambulance arrives.

READ

Read pages 10 and 11

Purpose: to find out if there is any more information to add to the mind map.

EXPLORE

Pause at page 11

Is there any information on this page that we have not put down in our mind map?

Do the captions give any extra information?

The Air **AMBULANCE**

The Air Ambulance can reach places that a road ambulance can't. It can also get to places very quickly. Sometime the Air Ambulance is the quickest and only way to get a patient to hospital.

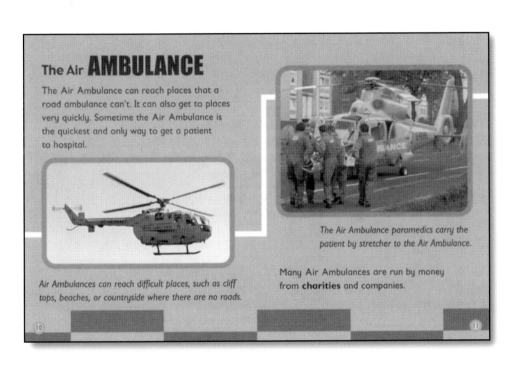

Air Ambulances can reach difficult places, such as cliff tops, beaches, or countryside where there are no roads.

The Air Ambulance paramedics carry the patient by stretcher to the Air Ambulance.

Many Air Ambulances are run by money from **charities** and companies.

READ

Read pages 12 and 13

Purpose: to find out if there is any more information to add to the mind map.

EXPLORE

Pause at page 13

Is there any information on this page that we have not put down in our mind map?

Speaking and Listening

Why has the author chosen to call this section 'Back to School'?

What does the glossary say about 'equipment'?

What would be some of the equipment used by the Ambulance Service?

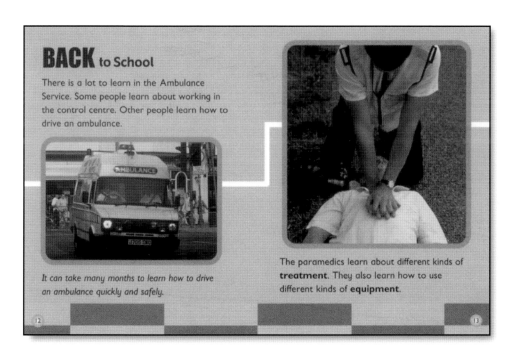

BACK to School

There is a lot to learn in the Ambulance Service. Some people learn about working in the control centre. Other people learn how to drive an ambulance.

It can take many months to learn how to drive an ambulance quickly and safely.

The paramedics learn about different kinds of **treatment**. They also learn how to use different kinds of **equipment**.

READ

Read pages 14 to 15

Purpose: to find out if there is any more information to add to the mind map.

EXPLORE

Pause at page 15

How can you turn the heading into a question?

What is the answer to the question?

HOW You Can Help the Ambulance Service

- Move out of the way if you see an ambulance with its lights flashing, or you hear its **siren** sounding.

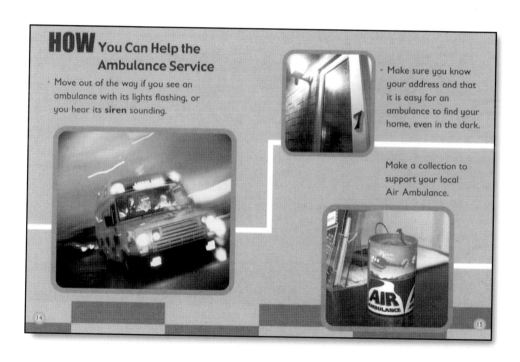

- Make sure you know your address and that it is easy for an ambulance to find your home, even in the dark.

Make a collection to support your local Air Ambulance.

Read page 16

Purpose: to use a glossary.

Pause at page 16

I'm going to read out a definition from the glossary. Can you tell me what the word being explained is? Let's try another.

Speaking and Listening

Now can you think of how to define 'ambulance'?

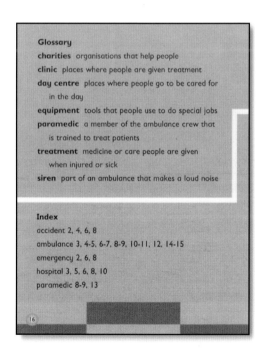

Glossary

charities organisations that help people

clinic places where people are given treatment

day centre places where people go to be cared for in the day

equipment tools that people use to do special jobs

paramedic a member of the ambulance crew that is trained to treat patients

treatment medicine or care people are given when injured or sick

siren part of an ambulance that makes a loud noise

Index

accident 2, 4, 6, 8

ambulance 3, 4-5, 6-7, 8-9, 10-11, 12, 14-15

emergency 2, 6, 8

hospital 3, 5, 6, 8, 10

paramedic 8-9, 13

16